Messag

from a

Jumbled Journey

and

Teeth, Tail,

Filigree, Garden and Sail

Caleb G.C. Jarvis

First published in 2001 by
Edward Gaskell *publishers*
Cranford House
6 Grenville Street
Bideford
Devon EX39 3DX

ISBN: 1 -898546 -46 -0

Messages
from a
Jumbled Journey

and

Teeth, Tail, Filigree
Garden and Sail

Caleb G.C. Jarvis

Designed, Printed & Bound by
Lazarus Press
Unit 7 Caddsdown Business Park
Bideford
Devon EX39 3DX

A Collection of Poems and Writitngs

Dedicated to

Those
Who Love

Lazarus Press

Contents

	Page
Ho Hum! - It's a Poets Life	11
Usual Muse	13
Reeling Toward	14
Dear Sir	15
All There Ever Was	16
To Plumb the Depth	17
Guitar Player In a Factory	18
Bothers to Boot	19
Open ye Mouth	20
A Factory Employee	21
Nature, Machines	22
I Have Fought In At Least Two Wars (you know)	23
The Gardener	24
In the Can	25
In Defence of Flowers	26
Are We United?	27
Amongst the Orientals and Before the Blue Tree	28
The Odd Couple	29
One More Hip To The Hurrah Of Christmas	30
A Descriptive Piece Of Writing	31
Toffee Apples	32
Lost Month	33
For You	34

Contents

	page
They Remind Me	35
The Face and The Muscle	36
I Love You	37
Towards the contrary-wise	38
What Two Eyes	39
Now It's Our time – Together We Smile	40
Whom Do I Love	41
I've Lost What I Found	42
On the Moment	45
For Lady	46
Christmas Cheer	47
Jolly Green Giant	48
By The Clothes I Wear	49
Thoughts in the Field	50
Thoughts of a Seemingly Empty Flat	52
The Sun Rocked	53
A Confusion of Thoughts During Sleep	54
Lady	55
I'm Out of Here	56
Is it this?	57
The Stale Flood	58
Number Tree	59
A Contemporary Poet Gathers Information	60
Sample 00 – Massively Interesting	62

Sausage burgers. Milk bun sandwiches. This is hell let loose on paper. The story of why *Messages From a Jumbled Journey* and *Teeth, Tail, Filigree, Garden and Sail* were written:

Briefly. . . . a young lady – when I was younger than I am now – introduced me to the works of Thomas Hardy.

I did not listen.

She introduced me to the music of a band called 'The Cure'.

I listened.

A year later I became near catatonic with the news that she was moving away. I was grieved by my social loss. Deeply grieved. Things were now in place for me to begin writing. A friend I felt had cared, I no longer understood (at least I had thought I *had* understood).

I wrote *Toffee Apples* a month later. I prayed to receive genius. My sub-conscious was primed. . . art became a potential saviour.

The following year my eyes studied a TV screen – apparently not switched on – broadcasting a crime programme from my psyche:

My crime?

The writing of *a letter* (the contents of which had committed the crime). LSD was my scapegoat . My life became an horrific fantasy movie.

In the early seventies a band called 'King Crimson' produced an album which they named *Earthbound*. They invited me to tour with them as a novel vocalist who sang *Twenty-First Century Schizoid Man* on stage.

In my hallucination I was five-years old. It was on the news, and my sub-conscious was writing the script. At one time I hallucinated nature-spirits – *or were they real?*

Hospital was my next domain. Revelations abounded.

Another lady, another life. More poems followed, composed through delusions of romance and crystallised undertones of reality with a sheen of fiction.

The theatre of the absurd,
coupled with a scandal-wrought social-link
amid lost documents and demo tapes
missing on the search for the bright side of Life.

Usual Muse

Blend of usual muse
sat on a desperate
edifice beyond

Pictorial being
visual space
withers thing

Astounding physique
pleasurably reveals
joyous sound

peacefully generating
sonic grace
thus forth

Reeling Toward

Reeling toward himself
many words that begin
spraints of thought

Exacting her own reality
pursuits arise

Peacefully a new world
washes with day break

Ensuring employment
expectations revealing glossy background
enormously a portrait of joy

"Dear Sir"

Fresh thoughts for Society:
People gleaning a second
image running through their
comical minds

Comtemplations of a better motion
creating a world so kind
generating a persona
for our people to remind
themselves of a golden time

Creating thoughts of good will
running as time, towards
a world as utopia
might be in mind

All There Ever Was

All there ever was
in mind
Alight confusion

All there ever was
in mind
a lack of self esteem

All there could be
was a head full
of truthful notions

And they would be
a head full of
insightful buttons
to communicate

To Plumb the Depth

To plumb the depth
of one's own mind
with all attempts
at being kind

So few of us actually
achieve what
it is to be normal,
practical and informed

When it comes to being
sociable without
frivolity and irresponsibilty
henceforth

When it comes to
normal behaviour
who is usually anyone's
saviour but one's self

Guitar Player in a Factory

The guitar player in a factory
never settles amongst
his own thoughts
maybe

This guitarist continued
to create music
in his subconscious

Ready for when he gets
home
to loveliness
whilst music exists
at work
in what's heard

Bothers to Boot

Bothers to boot
communication skills
up the shoot

Bothers to boot
We should listen
and could be helpful

Without pretence
to bother generous
aptitude without purpose

Open ye Mouth

Open ye mouth
and reveal your
state of mind

Reveal the state
of soul
upon the notion

Upon the
if ye subject yeself
of goodness knows

Open the airwaves
to love and rewarding
themes and music

A Factory Employee

A factory employee
adores an Icelandic
princess

A factory employee
adores a Scots Queen
up north

What does this mean
other than a
demoted aristocrat

Doing her duty
of course he is
What for two pints
of real love might be?

Nature, Machines

Nature, machines
amid the grand scheme
of things

To create an environment
that seems solid
and deems

Thing to be safe!

I have fought in at least two wars
(you know)

Stood am I by the water's edge
I dared do it - dredge up memories
of my last Love
how I felt joy when she smiled
from the tree branch above.
Now I have to go and fight another war.
A war situated outside another man's door
in a far off land.
I break the hour glass
to lay a durable road with sand.
Not now, my love
do I feel grand.
Mind spent
Body hovering
Lapsing to and from
one moment to the next
Disintegrating
Oh! why do we have to fight wars?
Sitting
Glaring
at a page
the raging, thrusting, thoughts
stop for a moment.
after reading a chapter title
I realise
I am entitled to my own identity

The Gardener

The gardener how he does chase
        the dying marigolds
He looks up and unfolds His fingers
from the piles of mutilated flowers
        and the smell that lingers
looking up into His love's face
it fills every space of His mind
how pleased He is to see her and
unbind
Himself from the sad work

In the Can

If you dry the standard of my life
the Can of my being will be shallow
Nonplussed
Give the wheels food
so that we may
stand amongst the Can
share sense
and non-prejudice
amongst the common

In Defence of Flowers

flowers are mis-handled
beaten down
stolen
left without water
to die
Dandelions taken and made into drinks
completely defenceless
Heat sensitive flowers
adjusting material quality
releasing elements of poison into their scent
this due to the change in atmosphere
Mutant flowers
later we find
Houseplants are protective
until altering their views
and our indecision
regarding their future

Are We United?

We are roaming around the living room
shouting
and bawling
As a row
until one realises
Things simmer down
saying
Can you stand me?
Yes
Bear our differences?
Yes
For the rest of our lives?
Yes
Allow me to play the stereo
after all it is respect you want?
No

I haven't watched TV since yesterday

Amongst the Orientals and Before the Blue Tree

She and I were walking slowly through an oriental
forest when the two of us were separated.
Also being closer to an actual unity I whispered my
thoughts.
These taught me to be passive when necessary.
Eventually I caught sight of my lost friend kneeling
before a blue tree while calling, saying:
Masses of orientals surround me
I questioned this not knowing where we were when
Man said:
Remember your lesson now you are on the path
We your friends hope the pair of you shall be
Equal
Passive

The Odd Couple

Here we are by the docks
near the sea
She thought love
was a simple affiliation, no.
But did he?
The man wondered was it an easy matter
to marry a woman
he tried to think.
Did she?
Each went on like this
treated each other courteously
The stress came
and the man wondered
if other women still.....
As did she about he
They parted
without revealing a grain of honesty

One More Hip To The Hurrah Of Christmas

Yet more days than a few
though less than many
I bring myself to think
About Christmas
Yet
again the word Yet
once more
I have thoughts
About Christmas
Even though we pledge
to change our ways in the new year
we remain as gullible as ever
A third time more the word Yet
and once more the word again
Christmas
Brings life to our minds
except for those who live the farce
without realising
there could be angels at work
I suppose I might as well add
One more Hip To The Hurrah Of Christmas

A Descriptive piece of writing

Wisps of alcohol vapour drift across the textured table
interacting with the plumes of blue-grey smoke
emitting from a stalk of ash held by a gripping finger.
Array raised light beams race around
the rim of glass
Chasing along curves
higher than the chin
From sips
drenched pores recline
sensation from drink
Senses
Taste
the complexions of these on skin of lips

Toffee Apples

Kiss the Trees
Kiss the Skies
Kiss Mother Nature
Sending love a sweet surprise
Loving the Trees Loving the Skies
Loving the Girl who greets
My Domain

Ò

The Lost Month

You left me in the Lost Month
standing alone in the crevice of an eternal heart
    Am crying
    A crowd try to usher me
    to a broken cart
    disheveled
    my ailing figure hangs
    Wondering
    what has been
    As I stand my eyes
    Melt
    into innumerable grains
    of silver sand
    before I sit
    my face
    Crumbles
    into one hand
    The other supports a frowning brow
    I try to think
    of you
    but my sour mind
    Rejects you
    anyhow
    I am paralysed
    until an afterthought
    Revives me
    paralysed until you touch me
    Before Dawn

For You

I would serenade from Venus

Paddle the seas on a tea leaf

In all kinds of weather

fly across mountains

by the aid of a humming bird feather

Cycle all the way from Mars

And stop Tokyo's traffic jams full of cars

If only you would come to my house

to chat, listen to music, and drink with me

They Remind Me

Here is the scent.
After travelling through the garden Mary says:

You are able to give one
a melancholic disposition.
I admire your beauty
but your power I fear.
Please disperse.
You fare well by the pretty standard
I want to feel fondness
but the flowers strangle
and detest romance
wanting to remind me
of when we parted
wanting to remind me
of the hardships

The Face and the Muscle

An oval ring
of sought-after experience
She
did not speak with her breasts
The muscles
surrounding those eyes
Those facial muscles
spoke
My appearance
made them say
that which I wanted to hear
I failed to understand
imagined there was passion
For a moment

I Love You

Here I am sitting
   looking through the book
                   that shook me
                   Yesterday

I smile as I lean forward
       and hear a voice say
                  I remember

I can hear you
   when I see you
       as I sit through
            the glittering fragments
                of memory
Pushing their way through to my face
   When I close my eyes I can see you
                As large as life
You're standing holding a scythe
  Reaping all the songs I shall write
  Tipping them into a basket of words
            Ready to leave my lips

    Like Black, Red and Yellow Birds

Towards the contrary-wise

I walked towards the girl
her eyelids the opposite of I
speaking to Mary I said
would you have me?
NO
was the reply
I am not well
might not be
until I die
could not love you as you please
do not wish to drag you down
with my disease,
show you consideration without love

Why not pray to the heavens above
who could twirl you in your steps
with her head in yours

What Two Eyes

When
I am not able to sleep
my eyes peep out
from the corner of my face
Stark Naked.
When
they encounter the human race
lids peeled back
It crosses my mind
That
If my eyes were to cease to function
the majority of my values and sensation
Would
shrivel away.
So from this day
I shall crave for my mind's eye
To be delivered from sin

So Now It's Our Time
(Together We Smile)

Time is moving
Moving we feel the wash of time against our faces
Together we drift through the endless waters
that suspend our mind
neither dreaming nor seeing
we climb
Marc Chagall says *Time is a River Without Banks*
I watch the empty faces peering through a window
She watches corpses bobbing toward us
The boat is listing
Nothing grabs at the oar keys
Our boat wades through the side alleys sheltering
good music, poetry and inspiration
I look at the faces without character
the vibrant souls without body
Chagall is watching
he says *There is a River Without Banks*
Now I realise
I have been all along without her
My life is empty
Together we smile

Whom Do I Love ?

Twilight bears a romantic silhouetted scene
Our gazes bounce from face to shoreline to sea
While gazing with leisure
upon a beautious neck
I am fixed with a ponderous curiosity
Whom Do I Love ?
I sit
The craggy light
emits from the gate of an unknown cavern
or aesthetic idols that I own
Is my heart to be torn and racked
with members of a broken unity?
Or will I fart with indifference
as my belief is kneaded
by a silken pummeling knee

Alone on a beach, I sat and had enough of wandering over, along and around. The very place I appear to have all of my own. Dropping the filling from a sandwich by no conscious wish. Sat looking at it thinking. . . .

mind now absent
Void
then an impression of a seagull
falters my nothingness
Eating the prawn & mayonnaise
and leaves
I am surprised and saddened
by the brilliant white that has gone
Head turning, head returning
Eyes alighten, mind is brightened
Long Beach, much sea
Crickety legs
 pins & needles in my feet

Stand up man!
calls the rising consciousness
Peep-Holes dotter the distance
receiving an impression
deep soul rising
beckons the necessary
from both bloodshot sleepless eyes
Left cerebrum aching
Is this energy I am faking
or is it real?

step by step by step
My soul is waiting ......
From one sad place
to the ease of a temporary bus-stop
another sad place
that cold flat
I remember it was a necklace
surfaced from a blazing
white-winged seagull
scrabbling for food

Now
over the road
are the blazing teeth
and elegant neck
I have never seen before
" Goodbye, Louise"
hums an inoculating voice
"Toodle-Pip Pat"
I trace the pendant
that should hang
about the elegant neck named Lady
" Hey! That Lady who wears the blazing teeth"
I called to her wits
other than the wits that hitched
and watched the narrowing road.
"Hey! Were you on the beach?"
"Why yes! Did you see me?"
"I saw someone I hoped was you"
"Did you lose a necklace?"
"You have found it?"

I smiled revealing white, yellow & groggy teeth
My stubble glistened in the winter sun
"You are very kind," Louise replied to my trampled
smile. "That pendant was a gift – a lost sentiment."

In the spring, on the bus, I was with memories of
a lost sentiment. Also I imagined in the distance
– from the past – a face. It reminded me of
a stained-glass window or a jewel. A certain
feeling of romance, lame and gone. The bus stop.
The face was there, recollections of the name
I had none. In awe and fear of beauty I
remembered Louise. The bus-stop. The face.
The sad place. The giving of what was and now
is none. That is the sad place where I sit after
wandering.

On the Moment

On the word
On the moment
She heard all I had to say
It was, I said, me.
Loved you from the very first
Have not your pretty eyes woken up to me yet
I will not bet
and I should not ponder
I should think
and not wonder
Whether you still love me
I was told by the wayside
Still
I wonder
to decide

?

For Lady

∞_∞∞
Lady
Your face suits my vision
we live in the state
of one which is distant
Our knowledge is imperfect
I do not know what to say to you
How about you
to me

Christmas Cheer

For the arrangements
I have made
this is not
the engagement
I could have proposed
to be said
Unfortune is not mine
I may dine another year
without feminine verbs
for my ear.
Though the fortune of another
disgraced love affair
is not mine to bear,
I wish somebody was here.

Jolly Green Giant

Conveying goodness that
greets truth with a grin
My clothes are honest
it is not a test
by what I wear accept another development
of what is within
Trousers of green canvas
This is what is seen on Earth
the colour of the leaves and grass
felt by heart and found by eye
enigmatic hues
colours
that is why people differ
what they don't understand
is understood by another

By the clothes I wear

It appears to help your mind move for or against.
What was thought once is now only whence
– more respected.
Others hope me to wear garments that cost
more than a few pounds and many more pence.
To their taste, even if I don't,
they say 'he is in want of taste'.
To me self-interest, like them,
the best, is no more special than the rest.
Different values, another personal test.
Fashionable clothes are a waste to workmen
in oily places, through weekly work races.
Besides, what is the case?
Handsome – for a painted face?
By harmful hearts, who'd depart
when affronted by honest soul trying
to overcome taintedness within opinion.
Is perhaps
goodness that wins?

Thoughts in the Field

Lady spoke, while the air was sweet, her breath soft
on Young Man's cheek.
These very puffs spoke this :
I am your Bathsheba Everdene
and you are my Gabriel Oak
A swing from illiterate force. He wished to know what
she meant. The gist given of her thought.
Lady asked :
Have you read
the book I mention?
Stubbornly, Young Man replied :
No.
What's more, books are boring

Further in the day Lady's field of ambition widened.
The Lady and her Lover :
Take my hand
Young Man, one third wish – one third not under-
standing. The remainder was spent not knowing how
to conduct himself.

Delicate tapering wisps of curling fingers rest on a bare tailor–model's hand.

Lady strove, as her name spells.
He'd begun to realise this Lady's portent.

Take my hand

Young Man, one third wish – one third not understanding. The remainder was spent not knowing how to conduct himself.

Delicate tapering wisps of curling fingers rest on a bare tailor–model's hand.

Lady strove, as her name spells. Young Man had begun to realise this Lady's portent.

Thoughts of a seemingly empty flat

Sat amongst the shambles
in a shambling posture
trying to condense
shambling thoughts.
That lady sat in the drifting blue car
eyes no longer wandering
pupils are fixed
on perhaps my hardly-clothed body
These eyes I own studying the ovulating red
printing the syllables of Love
in the air
until disappearing behind the bus-shelter wall

The Hendrix song :

Gypsy eyes are coming back

My thoughts assisted
by other persuasions
wishing the given syllables of Love
were printed on my tense jaw
I feel like praying to the Lord

Allow My Love
To become reality

Was that a celebrity?
or not?
Maybe her ghost is after me
perhaps to envelope my soul .....

The Sun Rocked......

amidst the motion of my glasses.

I wished to approach
a desirable person
of female gender
equipped with a potion of language.

I now desire the effect to be forgotten
and wish I could retrieve
the heart rent
during romantic collision.
her mind spent
and my soul
unkempt

Forgiveness is to be asked.

A Confusion of Thoughts During Sleep.

In the front-room of my flat, I am knelt
beside an electric heater   a head resting
on a pair of shoulders
both belong to the edifice of bodiliness.
Whose are they ? You may ask. Why if
this particular piece of writing is about
himself, is it becoming a script , in this
fashion?

An out of body experience perhaps.
Or is the reason that mischief is in mind?

' So he is clever, hey,
writing in this manner of gibberish?
He won't get no 'O' level in English
Not never, not by writing at the
end of his essay "and now is the end
of the story, as I've ran out of space". '
Or did he?

  Note : 'Cleverness does not suit him'
                                         Teach.

54

Lady

A sister in God
May your handsome feet
be shod
by boots of soul fortune
let the Lord speak
for my testimony is weak
Soul. . . Disturbed. . .Ugly Life. . .
Art in Mind. . . Forgive Me. . .
Residing Within is an Aesthete
plus fancies
Yes. A mind with a touch of sin
let me/you/speaker/audience
in view
of an angel's mind.
I pray that we bind
our bodies
are
one

I'm out of Here

There was a room
It is dark

He was looking in
Outside is light

The woman stares out
Inside her they say is dark

In him is said to be life
He beckons her out

What, is the answer

Why not?
When there is light and life before you

She says
I want sex

I pledge happiness
for both TV and Radio

Now it is
incredible

I'm out of here

as she leaps out

still he beckons

Is it this?

Heart break
Part make
But I am the one
Who does shun
others
As others shun me
I have broken (their) hearts
I part make
say hello
not intending to take.
As I do, I do
there are those who
do to me
what I do to you
Is it seen?
is it really this?
Times come when I wish
often in my life

The Stale Flood

There, stood in the corner
was a girl
I wanted to warn her
of the everlasting flood
She wondered about the blood
in both her wrists
This flood was actually an emotion
of urgent need
an uncontrolled pitiful greed
for another
lover
was now alone
and pleased
How could she
be appeased
Without crying

Number Tree

sing tree, marry again, sin, forgive us god
marry again give or take
sing for me
i shall sing for you
under the elm tree
which is diseased
like my love for you

. . . and your love for me

shall we marry again?
or will it be seen as a sin
against the lord
or you
or me
shall
we
forgive us
or will we
be forgiven
we two

A Contemporary Poet
Gathers Information

Well. . . I'm sitting on my bed, once more tapping away on the keys of an old typewriter which just happens to belong to me – not rented you see.

The message has plenty of content.

One story of mine describes, through circumlocution, details of my rented room with its chrokium plated towel rail. Chrokium?

How odd could the word chromium eventually sound if I were to keep mis-spelling it. I wonder. . .

I suppose (metaphorically speaking) it would look like the masochist who kept asking to be beaten up and tortured.

Or, alternatively this self-contorted word could well be a sadist wanting to torture its readers.

Now this is what I wish to talk to you about, these two human phenomena of attitude – The 'Inflicting' sadist and the 'Afflicted' masochist.

Now. . . the sadist doesn't appear to feel guilt and the masochist (possibly) could not sense sorrow without gaining something from it.

These two little oddments I gathered from my own experiences.

I've abused as well as been a victim. I used to head butt. Hard. Also I would punch and kick without remorse, said Man.

Then it happened and I became an emotional masochist. This, of course, was after I became a victim. The two main causes of my affliction were: The ignorance of elders (as well as contemporaries and youngers) and Nature as it stands (an inability to be understood until after the event).

I remember being punched so hard in the face that the framed lenses on my face flew off to the left of me and blood spurted on to the floor and wall over five feet away. I think, that when this happened, a thrill went through me – though later I was much upset concerning the whole business. Traumatic as the incident was I am still able to reflect and learn from it. Also, I am fascinated by my own mental illness. Having once been deluded in a floral fashion (that is, meaning bizarre) my mind is well-enough equipped to be interested in itself. Not only for moral fabrication – but also curiousness.

For instance...

"Oh! Louise, you wondrous being. Thoe [actually I mean those] curly locks of jet long hair. Your cute nose and sweet looking lips. And also your pleasant sense of dress. Now I write you poems of Love, and letters of sensitivity – all of which is not enjoyed, appreciated, nor wanted by you. In the art room both of us [do you know I actually mean *us*] were spirits at work in the same school, but with differing directions."

Yes! I would be sat at home writing letters to my sparkling wonder.

She told me to. . . think again.

Sample 00

Massively interesting

Massively interesting; well that's what he thought *william sprespore* considered sincerely as an opinion upon matters relatively distant from his own wealth of knowledge owing to the fact of which *anderson spotsworse* unduly disregarded all points of related actuallity of experimental duty. . .

oh. . . for God's sake!

Down the corridor, between the tree's displacing ephemeral shafts of ethereal bible bee beams, thoughts burbling, a certain delusive quality of visual tendancy through a flashy flickering black box of glittery colours for your amusement, if you are so inclined. Perforce, *john twiddlebum de stinslur* belching a ruling note somewhere over there, (for your amusement, even if you are not so inclined).

Aspects of thought instinctively answering then, when they begin, also being now, after any instigation of other aspects within thought's outside the centre inside the periphery over the edge, and under the stairs of your friend's daydream, while you were asleep, someone said in passing to a retired bus-driver something you seem to recollect thinking the other day, or was it *deja vu*, despite the two hour-long lecture in law whilst having heard that fascinating passage next to you.

Massively interesting, the rancid doctor said, as *dolly spivworth* sat splicing toe nails onto depleting eye brows of adot potty being deconded itself, whilst deciding what it could grow into next, after having decayed for some years worth of retrospective self – through generations past, generations now, and not forgotting, generations to arise during general decisions of specific time value, if you like?